Heroes
Who Live On

Volume 2

© 2005 by BMH Books
P.O. Box 544
Winona Lake, IN 46590
1-800-348-2756
www.bmhbooks.com

For more information on the Fellowship of Grace Brethren Churches:
    www.fgbc.org
    www.fgbcworld.com
    www.cenational.org

ISBN 0-88469-083-0

All rights reserved. No part of this publication may be reproduced, stored in a retrieval system, or transmitted in any form or by any means—electronic, mechanical, photocopy, recording, or any other—except for brief quotations in printed reviews, without the prior permission of the publisher.

Unless otherwise indicated, Bible quotations are taken from the New International Version, Copyright © 1973, 1978, 1984 by International Bible Society

Scripture quotations marked NASB are from the New American Standard Bible®, Copyright © 1960, 1962, 1963, 1968, 1971, 1972, 1973, 1975, 1977, 1995 by The Lockman Foundation. Used by permission. www. Lockman.org

Scripture quotations marked KJV are from the Holy Bible, King James Version, 1611.

Writers/Editors: Robert Cover, Sr., Viki Rife, Ashley Woodworth
Sketches and Cover Design by Sarah Pratt

Contents

Preface

This book is the second volume of a project that was begun at CE National in Winona Lake, Indiana, under the direction of its executive director, Ed Lewis.

It is based on the conviction that children can learn character through the example of others. Like Volume 1, this volume includes stories of people who did not set out to be heroes—they simply followed God as they understood His Word and as they ministered in the context of the Grace Brethren family of churches.

Usually we think of heroes as the biggest, the best, the strongest, and the smartest. Even the way they dress identifies them as heroes. We would love to be like them, and we like to pretend we *are* them. Compared to what they accomplish, our own lives seem insignificant. We look up to them and admire them, realizing we will never be able to do the things they do.

God knows all about heroes. But His standards for hero status are different from ours. The people in *Heroes Who Live On* did not know they were heroes. They just did what God showed them to do. It was mostly hard work and good Christian living.

The world around them often didn't understand what they were doing. In that sense, they fit in well with God's heroes described in Hebrews 11. Like Moses, they "persevered because they saw him who is invisible" (v. 27).

They persevered. They hung in there, doing what was right in God's eyes. Of course, we don't know exactly how every conversation went, or the small details of their lives, but these stories are based on historical facts and what we know about their character.

Each person whose story is told in this book believed God, focused on Him, and finished well. Right up until their deaths, these *spiritual ancestors* persisted. Because they chose to keep following God, they are true heroes.

Their lasting contributions to the Fellowship of Grace Brethren Churches are significant. Their investment in peoples' lives, in churches, and in national movements will live on for many years.

They have all gone to be with the Lord, so for many, we have no way of recapturing exact details of their lives or their thinking. Most chapters are based on a combination of published works, personal remembrances, and interviews with people who knew them and their activities.

Dialogue has been added to bring color and life, and to make the story interesting for young readers. Discussion questions following each chapter are designed to help Sunday School classes and small groups reflect on the character of the subjects, to think about applicable Scriptures, and to envision ways to model the featured virtues in daily life.

Our prayer with this volume, as with the first, is that the spirit of each person featured will shine through these stories and that a new generation of leadership will be inspired to imitate them by imitating Christ.

We do not want you to become lazy, but to imitate those who through faith and patience inherit what has been promised (Hebrews 6:12).

Henry R. Holsinger

Henry R. Holsinger
1833–1905

Henry R. Holsinger

Publisher

How beautiful on the mountains are the feet of those who bring good news, who proclaim peace, who bring good tidings, who proclaim salvation, who say to Zion, "Your God reigns!" (Isaiah 52:7).

Publisher: dedicated to making God's truth available to all

Susanna Holsinger stood in the doorway, looking at the man leaning carefully over a large tray full of metal pieces. In his hand he held a smaller tray. He would look up at a piece of paper posted in front of him, then reach into the large tray, choose a small block of metal, and place it in the small tray. Then he would choose another, and then another, carefully lining them up side by side.

Susanna glanced around the room. Paper was stacked along the walls. Handwritten notes were tacked everywhere. In the center of the room stood a huge structure, with a large steel pressing plate and rubber rollers. She smiled. They had saved so long to buy that printing press, and finally, it was here. Her husband looked so happy as he prepared the type for his newsletter.

In 1884 there were no computers or photocopiers. The only way to make a copy of something was either to copy it by hand or set it for printing. This involved arranging small pieces of metal with letters on them (called "type") and locking them into a frame that could be mounted on the printing press. Then a roller with ink on it would run across the letters, and a piece of paper would be pressed onto the inked letters. When removed, the paper would have the imprint of the letters, much like using a rubber stamp today. Although it was a complicated process compared to today's printing methods, it was still better than writing something over and over by hand.

"Henry," Susanna said softly. Her husband looked up.

"Don't you want some supper?" she asked.

Henry sighed. "Let me just finish this paragraph," he said. "I really want to get the project done tonight." He quickly added the letters for the last few words. Then he walked over to his wife and put his arm around her.

"Susanna," he said, as they walked toward the dining room, "I'm worried about our children. What are we doing to prepare them to serve God in the future?"

Susanna stopped and looked at him in surprise. "Henry, I think we've done quite well with Annie and Lottie," she replied.

"Oh, I didn't mean just our own children," Henry said quickly. "You've done a wonderful job of working with them. I mean the children in all our churches. Sometimes we adults get so wrapped up in our church problems we forget to see that our children learn what they need to know about living for Jesus. They will be the leaders of our churches someday—shouldn't we be doing something to train them now?"

"But what can we do?" asked Susanna. "We can't travel to all the churches to train the children. You're the pastor of our own church. Besides, we just bought the printing press so you could print newsletters to send to the churches. You know they help the churches a lot."

Henry sighed. Susanna was right. They couldn't leave the responsibilities they already had. Suddenly, his eyes widened. He grabbed her hands. "Susanna, that's it!" he exclaimed. "We could start a newsletter for children! It would be a wonderful way to communicate with them and give them a chance to express themselves. They could write in with their questions and suggestions."

4

Susanna could see that her husband's mind was already organizing his ideas for the newsletter. "It's a great idea," she said excitedly. "Maybe Lottie would like to help you."

Soon the first issue of *The Pious Youth,* a newsletter designed especially for children and young people, was being sent to the churches. The children loved having their own newsletter.

Lottie enjoyed helping her father with the newsletter. A club was started for the children who received the newsletter. Lottie invited children to send their pennies to help with certain needs in some of the churches. The children who helped out called themselves the Dewdrop Mission Club, picturing each penny as a drop of dew that would eventually fill a bucket. In each issue of the newsletter, Lottie would let them know how many pennies had come in.

People in the churches started to see that children really were interested in serving God. One elder, Joe Beer, wrote to the *Evangelist,* the magazine Henry Holsinger was publishing for the churches. "I want to start a Band of Hope," he said. "If you say that you will not drink any intoxicating liquor as a beverage, that you will not chew or smoke tobacco, and that you will try to do your best to use no profane words, I want you to send me your name, your age, and the post office address." He added, "I will write all such names in a pretty little book which I call the *Band of Hope Book of Remembrance.*

Soon many children were joining a "Band of Hope" in their church. In every issue of the magazine, "Uncle Joe" would answer children's letters.

One day a child wrote suggesting they should have badges to show that they had joined the Band of Hope. "Uncle Joe" didn't have enough money to send badges to all the children, but he suggested that they take blue ribbon and embroider yellow initials to represent the Band of Hope. Soon children were wearing their badges to show everyone that they had made a commitment to live for God.

Henry Holsinger's beginnings were far from those of a publisher. He had started out as a farmer and carpenter in western

Pennsylvania. His parents had been able to give him, as he described it, "only the commonest of a common-school education" in those days when only people who could afford it went to school regularly. But in 1856, Henry took a job as a printer's apprentice, or helper. He began to see the power of printed words to communicate ideas. In 1863 he purchased his own newspaper printing company, and used his paper to report what was happening during the Civil War.

What really mattered to Henry, though, was spreading the truth about Jesus. He sold his newspaper in 1873 and became the pastor of a church in Berlin, Pennsylvania. He still wanted to help other churches, so he started a magazine called the *Christian Family Companion.* Some of the leaders in the churches became upset because he said some things they were doing weren't right. Finally, they recommended that Henry Holsinger should be "disfellowshiped,"—not allowed to be part of the church.

Henry and others who shared his concerns tried to find a peaceful solution. Finally, they realized they would need to start their own church. In 1883 they organized The Brethren Church, often called the "progressive" group.

Everyone looked to Henry to lead the group. He wisely helped the Progressive churches to keep their focus on what was important. He also made many sacrifices of his own time and money to travel among the churches to encourage them and to support the idea of a Christian college for young people. The travel and stress weakened his health.

Henry's last great work was *The History of the Tunkers and the Brethren Church,* which is still recognized as a classic book of Brethren history. Much of the book was dictated to a secretary, though Henry often had to stop trying to speak and just point to words, since his voice and strength were failing. The book was finished in 1901.

Henry sold most of what he owned to pay for printing the book. To his disappointment, it did not make money for him.

However, many people today have a better understanding of Brethren history because of his careful research and recording of God's faithfulness.

Henry Holsinger's life was inspired by the simple dedication of the first Brethren believers who left their homes in Schwarzenau, Germany, to travel to the United States, where they could serve God as they believed they should. Henry described this inspiration in his book:

> "How often they must have battled with the homesick feeling that will come to all who love home and leave it! How often in their dreams their feet pressed again the grassy slopes of the Eider, they drank again of its crystal water, and breathed again the pure mountain air, and were happy again in their old homes, only to wake to find it all a dream! These brave men and women endured much so that they might serve the Lord in His own appointed way. …Shall we not be true to the cause we have espoused, and for which our fathers suffered much, yea, for which Christ died? God help us to be faithful even unto death." *(History of the Tunkers, pp. 42–43)*

Questions for Discussion

1. Henry Holsinger had a passion for spreading the gospel. Can you think of some biblical characters who also told others the way of salvation?

2. Not everything we read is true. How do we know God's Word is true?

3. The children in the "Band of Hope" said they would not smoke, drink, or use bad language. Could you commit to that, too? Is there anything else you could add?

L. S. Bauman

L. S. Bauman
1875–1950

L. S. Bauman

Leadership

Be diligent in these matters; give yourself wholly to them, so that everyone may see your progress. Watch your life and doctrine closely. Persevere in them, because if you do, you will save both yourself and your hearers (1 Timothy 4:15–16).

Leadership: the ability to inspire others by example

Little Paul Bauman watched as his papa welcomed the visitors to their home. Papa had told him that these were very important people. Paul was used to his father having important people come to the house, because Papa was well known in Brethren churches.

Paul started to go in with them to the room where they were meeting. Then he stopped. Papa said he needed to talk about something important with these people, and told Paul he could not stay for the conversation.

Paul turned around and ran into the kitchen. He opened the silverware drawer and pulled out a fork. Then he ran through the door of the room where Papa and the guests were meeting. Papa looked over and started to tell him not to come in. Paul was too fast. He ran up to Papa, held up the fork clutched in his fist, and stabbed his daddy's leg as hard as he could.

The visitors gasped. Paul stood still, looking up at his father. Dr. Bauman smiled faintly at his son. "Run along, Paul," he said calmly. Then he reached down and pulled the fork out of his leg.

Paul smiled to himself as he left the room. It was so funny to watch the horrified faces of the visitors! Paul knew the secret that Papa was now explaining to his guests. Papa's leg was an artificial one made of cork. He had lost his real leg in a farming accident long ago.

It wasn't his cork leg that had made Paul's father, Louis S. Bauman, great or famous. Dr. Bauman was known among Brethren people for his preaching, his wisdom, and the way he taught the Bible. He had accepted Jesus as his Savior when he was 11 years old, not long after he lost his leg. Soon after that he wrote his first article. It was published in a magazine called *The Brethren Evangelist.*

Before long, Louis Bauman started preaching. He was so young that people called him "The Boy Preacher." Years after he had become a pastor and a conference speaker, his mother told him, "Son, before you were two hours old I lifted you in my arms and dedicated you to the Lord for Christian ministry." God had heard the prayers of this faithful mother.

After serving as pastor of churches in Indiana and Illinois, Louis Bauman was asked to become pastor of the First Brethren Church in Philadelphia. Living in such a major city gave him an opportunity to meet many of America's leading Bible teachers and preachers.

While he was in Philadelphia, Louis became more and more concerned about people who had never had an opportunity to hear the message of Jesus. He worked hard to help plan a new missionary work in Argentina. He also became interested in reaching people in Persia (now Iraq and Iran). He lived in a three-story house, so he decided to rent the third floor of his home to Persian students who had come to Philadelphia to study. This gave him a chance to know more about Persia.

In everything he did, Louis Bauman had the vision to look past difficulties and see opportunities to reach people for Christ. He believed if God showed someone what needed to be done, that person should act immediately. His life motto, which any-one who heard him preach can remember, was, "It's in the Book! What are you going to do about it?"

One person who accepted Christ in Dr. Bauman's church was a young streetcar conductor named James Gribble (see *Heroes, Vol. 1).* James was convinced that God wanted him to go to the center of Africa, to tribes who had never heard about Jesus. Dr. Bauman explained to James that the Brethren Church did not have a mission in Africa, and he encouraged him to pray. James found another mission that would send him to Kenya.

Eight years later James came back, now with a wife and two-year-old daughter. Again he went to Dr. Bauman and explained that he wanted to reach people who had never heard the message of Jesus.

Dr. Bauman sighed. "James," he said, "do you understand what you're asking? There is no established mission where you want to go. There are no other missionaries. There are no government representatives in the area to protect you from the fierce tribes. Some of them are head-hunters and cannibals! There's a war going on right now, and it just isn't wise to take a ship across the Atlantic Ocean. You have to get permission from the French to enter that area, and they aren't likely to give it to their own people, much less to you. Besides, it's not a place to take a small child."

Then Dr. Bauman smiled at James. "I know you and your wife are people of faith. If you pray and prepare yourselves to go, I promise that our church will support you. I'll ask others to help you, too." With those words of encouragement, the Gribbles began to prepare to go to the center of Africa. Because of their pioneer work there, that land now has about 900 established churches, with about 230,000 baptized believers.

Dr. Bauman had married Mary Wageman, a lively, energetic woman who loved helping him with his church. They had three children—Paul was the youngest. When little Paul was only 18 months old, a serious flu virus infected many people in the area. Mary and the oldest boy, who was six years old, both died.

Their deaths were a terrible blow to Louis. He began to wonder what God was doing in his life. As he struggled to take care of two little children who now had no mother, he turned to God's Word for comfort. The more he studied his Bible, the more interested he became in prophecy, which showed how God was working in the world. When he started preaching again, he became one of the best-known speakers on prophecy, speaking in Bible conferences throughout the country.

Eventually he became pastor of the "Fifth and Cherry" Brethren Church in Long Beach, California. He served at that church for 34 years. Through his influence, many young people dedicated their lives to serving God in places all over the world.

He was a leader in the Brethren Foreign Missionary Society for many years, and also helped start Grace Theological Seminary. He was instrumental in helping clarify the theological controversies that led to the split with the Ashland Brethren and the founding of the Fellowship of Grace Brethren Churches in the late 1930s.

Dr. Bauman made it a point to write letters to encourage people throughout the world. Even though he was a busy man and traveled a lot, he loved his family. He and his son Paul were very close. One postcard that Paul kept the rest of his life showed a man riding an ostrich. His father had written, "Dear Little Boy, Last night and all day today I spent with a man I have known ever since I was a little boy like you…We were out at the ostrich farm today. How would you like to have a horse like this one? This will be my last card to you from Los Angeles. Be a good boy. Don't forget to mind Auntie. Lovingly, Papa."

Dr. Bauman was 73 years old when he went to be pastor of the First Brethren Church in Washington, D.C., but his writing ministry continued. Although he had written thousands of articles for Christian magazines, including the *Brethren Missionary Herald,* he kept writing. Even when he had to be in a wheelchair, he still wrote articles and letters. In one of his last letters he said, "The Lord's coming seems so very near, that I almost feel His breath upon my cheek." He was buried on his 75th birthday in Germantown, Pennsylvania.

Questions for Discussion

1. Sometimes bad things happen to good people. Louis lost his wife and first son. Can you think of biblical characters who also lost loved ones? Did they respond like Louis, finding comfort in God?

2. Louis' motto, "It's in the Book! What are you going to do about it?" showed he believed the Bible tells us how to live. Can you think of passages in the Bible that give us instructions for living?

3. Louis was a leader who began preaching and writing at a young age. How can you be a leader for Jesus right now?

Mary Bauman

Mary Bauman
1876–1909

Mary Bauman

Nurture

Let the little children come to me, and do not hinder them, for the kingdom of heaven belongs to such as these (Matthew 19:14).

Nurture: to help or promote the development of healthy growth

Lida walked quietly into the crowded church, trying to stretch tall enough to find a place to sit. She was so excited she could hardly stand it. Finally she was twelve, old enough to be a part of the Christian Endeavor Society! It was the only organization in her church that allowed young people to be members.

This was her very first meeting. Where should she sit? As she made her way through the crowd, she heard someone calling her name. Mrs. Bauman was motioning to an empty seat beside her. Lida scooted onto the hard wooden pew. The only thing better than finally being a part of the Christian Endeavor Society was getting to sit by Mary Bauman, the young, fun-loving wife of their new pastor.

Their church at Third and Dauphin streets in Philadelphia had changed a lot when the Baumans came. Louis and Mary Bauman were young and full of fun. Mr. Bauman preached God's Word with enthusiasm. When they sang, Mrs. Bauman's beautiful voice helped them sing harmony parts. The Baumans loved to have people over to their house. They even played games with the young people. As Lida later said, "We felt like we were in the hands of friends."

While this may not seem unusual to us, back in the early 1900s it was very unusual. Pastors often kept their distance from the rest of the people in the church, partly because it was considered undignified for a pastor to laugh and play games, but also because people in the church did not want the pastor to know what their lives were really like. People tried to be on their best behavior for the pastor. Sometimes they didn't even know their pastor's first name, because they never used it.

But it was hard to be stiff and dignified with the Baumans around. They seemed to believe that living for Jesus was fun, and their joy was contagious. They were excited about helping people know the Bible and God better. They had a warm, friendly way of looking you in the eye as if you really mattered, even if you were only twelve years old.

Lida listened quietly as the service began. It wasn't long before she started to realize, however, that the only important people in the Christian Endeavor Society were the ones who were over 50 years old. They were the ones who got up and spoke to the rest of the group on the topic of the day. They were the ones who prayed out loud. Lida began to feel very young, immature, and insignificant as she listened to experienced Christians tell how they were serving God.

"I don't want to wait until I'm fifty years old to serve God," Lida thought to herself. "Surely there must be something someone my age can do."

As the meeting ended, Lida saw that Mrs. Bauman had been watching her. She felt as if Mrs. Bauman could see right through her, yet she didn't feel embarrassed. "She really cares about me," Lida thought. Just then Mrs. Bauman leaned over.

"Can you come over to my house tomorrow night after supper?" she whispered. "I'll invite some other girls, too. Bring your Bible."

The next morning Lida's friend Susan stopped by to walk to school with her. As soon as Lida came out the door, Susan exclaimed, "Lida, guess what! Mrs. Bauman asked me last night if I could come to her house to meet with some other girls. Are you going?"

All day in school Lida could hardly concentrate. Why would Mrs. Bauman invite a bunch of girls to her house? What did she have in mind?

That night, Lida and Susan hurried down the street as fast as they could. They both had remembered to bring their Bibles.

"I have an idea," Mrs. Bauman said to the twelve girls who gathered in her living room. "Let's organize a Sisterhood of Mary and Martha."

The girls looked at her questioningly. "What does that mean?" they asked.

She had them turn in their Bibles to Luke 10:38–42. "Let's read it out loud together," she suggested.

> "As Jesus and his disciples were on their way, he came to a village where a woman, named Martha, opened her home to him. She had a sister called Mary, who sat at the Lord's feet listening to what He said. But Martha was distracted by all the preparations that had to be made. She came to Him and asked, 'Lord, don't you care that my sister has left me to do the work by myself? Tell her to help me!'
>
> 'Martha, Martha,' The Lord answered, 'you are worried and upset about many things, but only one thing is needed. Mary has chosen what is better, and it will not be taken away from her.'"

"You see," Mrs. Bauman explained, "we all have some of Mary and some of Martha in us. We can worship God, like Mary did. But we can serve God, too, like Martha served Jesus. We can help each other learn to balance those two important parts of our lives."

The girls began to talk excitedly. What could they do to serve God?

"We could bake cookies for old Mrs. Groaty. We could even take them to her ourselves, and sing for her."

"We could offer to go to the grocery store for Mrs. Donaldson."

"We could pray for people that we know, and for our friends who don't know Jesus."

"We could collect money to help the missionaries, too."

Mrs. Bauman gave them all an encouraging, satisfied smile. "I knew you girls would be willing to help. What should our motto be?"

One of the girls looked back at the Bible on her lap. "I noticed that Jesus said, 'Only one thing is needed.' That could be our motto."

Mrs. Bauman nodded her head thoughtfully. "You're right. The most important thing is learning what Jesus has to say to us."

Soon the girls were meeting every Sunday morning before the church service for special devotions together. Once a month they went to the Baumans' home to spend time together and plan how they would serve others. For Lida, her times with Sisterhood of Mary and Martha, or SMM, as they began to call it, were exciting.

The group started in 1906. Soon other Brethren churches saw what was happening and wanted to start an SMM group of their own. In 1913 SMM became a national organization of the Brethren church, which grew until there were more than 2,500 girls involved.

Dr. Florence Gribble (see *Heroes, Vol. 1*), who was a missionary doctor in Africa, wrote a letter to the SMM girls. She didn't have money to buy bandages for her patients. She was wondering if the girls could take old, worn-out sheets, tear them into strips, sew them together, and roll them up to send to her. She could use them as bandages for her patients.

The girls were very excited about this new project to help others. They collected sheets, then spend an evening together, chatting and laughing as they rolled bandages. They called the girl who rolled the most bandages the "Bandage Queen." Soon the groups were even selecting a national Bandage Queen. The girls had good times working together on the bandages and packing them into barrels to send to Africa.

Mary Bauman didn't live to see SMM become a national organization, or to see all the ways that SMM girls would serve others over the years. She died in 1909 during a flu epidemic. But she had started something that would affect the lives of thousands of girls. Even today, girls can learn to worship and serve God through SMM.

Questions for Discussion

1. Mary Bauman nurtured the willing spirit in young girls by giving them opportunities to help others. Can you think of a younger sibling or friend you can nurture?

2. Martha was busy when Jesus came. It is very easy to be so busy that we forget to spend time with Jesus. How can we regularly spend time with Jesus?

3. Lida said the Baumans were friendly and fun. Can you think of ways to be friendly and fun in your church?

R. Paul Miller

R. Paul Miller
1891–1964

R. Paul Miller

Soul Winner

Preach the Word; be prepared in season and out of season; correct, rebuke and encourage—with great patience and careful instruction" (2 Timothy 4:2).

Soul Winner: committed to making sure everyone has an opportunity to hear the gospel

"Hey, Dan, where are you going?" Tim called down the street to his cousin.

"I'm going to hear the evangelist, R. Paul Miller," Dan shouted back.

"Why? My dad says preachers are just people who make a lot of money by telling stories. They don't really care whether anyone else goes to heaven." Tim laughed. "Dad says he's going to have fun now. He won't worry about God until he's old and dying."

"You mean, like Grandpa?" Dan said quietly.

Tim stopped laughing. A chill ran down his spine. Grandpa had always been their special buddy, taking them on camping and fishing trips, helping them make kites and toy sailboats. But two weeks ago the doctor had told the family that Grandpa didn't have very long to live. What if Grandpa really needed God? Tim hurried to catch up with Dan.

The service had already started when the boys entered the building. Tim enjoyed the singing, but his mind kept wandering.

He barely heard the evangelist start to preach. He was wondering what would happen to Grandpa after he died.

Suddenly, Tim noticed that people were getting up to leave. He couldn't see Dan anywhere. He was afraid to leave. If he moved, Dan would never find him.

Finally, he saw Dan coming toward him through the crowd, smiling the biggest smile Tim had ever seen.

"Where were you?" Tim asked irritably.

"I went to give my heart to God," said Dan. "He has taken away all my sins. And Tim, I asked that evangelist to go visit Grandpa and tell him how he can be saved, too."

"What? You're crazy. Why would Grandpa want to talk to this man? Besides, you know that preacher won't go. It's more than 10 miles to Grandpa's house."

"I gave him directions," said Dan. "I want Grandpa to hear about Jesus like I did tonight. That way he can go to heaven when he dies."

Tim started to argue, but something in Dan's face made him stop. He had always admired his older, more level-headed cousin. This seemed very important to Dan.

While the boys were walking home from the meeting, R. Paul Miller, the evangelist, was talking with the pastor of the church. "Do you know anything about this boy Dan whose grandfather is so sick?" he asked.

"Not really," the pastor answered. "I've seen him in the neighborhood a few times. But I don't know whether he really has a grandfather who's sick, or if he's just playing a joke."

"He gave me directions to the house," said Mr. Miller. "We really should go there, just in case this man really is dying. If we hurry, we can still get over to the station in time to catch my train by midnight."

They climbed into the pastor's car. Rev. Miller sank, exhausted, into the seat. He'd had a hard day. He always put a lot of energy into his preaching, and he had preached three times. He had been hoping to catch a quick nap before sitting up on a train the rest of the night.

A part of him just wanted to turn around. But he thought, "If I was dying, and didn't know Jesus, I would appreciate someone making the effort to come tell me how to be saved, no matter how tired he was." They kept going.

Finally they reached the house. Everything was dark. Obviously the family had gone to bed. What should they do? R. Paul Miller was determined to give this man a chance. They had come this far—they couldn't turn away now. They stumbled around in the dark, trying to find the door.

Suddenly, through the open window, they heard a voice call out, "Who's there?" They explained who they were. "I can't get up," said the voice. "The door's unlocked; just come in."

They found the door and opened it. When they switched on the light, there lay the sick man on a bed. "In 10 minutes we had read him the promises of God, and he had accepted them," said Rev. Miller years later as he told the story. "We had prayer with him and went on."

Rev. Miller made it in time to catch his train. One week later he got a letter from the pastor, telling him the man had died, rejoicing in Jesus his Savior.

R. Paul Miller was a true evangelist. It didn't matter whether he was speaking to a thousand people or to one—he just wanted everyone to have a chance to hear the truth of God's salvation. He had accepted Christ as his Savior when he was a boy, living in Los Gatos, near San Francisco, California. He was 15 when the city of San Francisco was hit by the great earthquake that almost destroyed it. A year later, both his mother and sister died. These hard times caused him to turn to God for comfort, strength, and wisdom.

After R. Paul's mother died, his father moved the family to southern California, among the orange groves and farms. Farming and gardening became some of R. Paul's favorite activities. God was preparing him for the challenge of caring for a family without a steady job.

R. Paul met Anne Meyers at church and they were married in 1914. He would take the Red Car electric train into the city to his classes at the Bible Institute of Los Angeles. When R. Paul graduated from BIOLA, he was called to pastor the Brethren church in Spokane, Washington. He enjoyed the beautiful, productive farmland, and continued his hobby of raising fruit trees. About five years later, he was asked to become an evangelist for the Brethren churches. The family moved back to southern California and R. Paul traveled all over the country, preaching the truth about Jesus in his strong, resonant voice.

Several years later, while preaching in Philadelphia, he was asked to become the pastor of the church there. He accepted. The family moved from southern California to a neighborhood where the houses were attached to each other. There was no front yard, just a sidewalk right outside the front door. The back yard was surrounded by a wooden fence. To the Miller children, it felt like they had moved to a foreign country.

Some time later the family moved again, this time to a farm in Berne, Indiana. There R. Paul taught his children to raise fruit and other crops. Sometimes it was hard being an evangelist. The churches would pay whatever they could afford for this traveling preacher who helped them tell their neighborhoods about Christ. R. Paul never knew how much he would get paid. The Great Depression was making life hard for everyone, and often the churches couldn't pay much at all. With ten children, it was very hard to keep everyone fed and clothed.

Sometimes the family would wait anxiously to see whether Dad would bring home enough to pay the family bills. There were times when R. Paul would say, "I couldn't bring much money, but go look in the car trunk." The trunk would be full of produce, salted meat, home-canned jam and preserves, and other basic foods.

According to the Miller children, their father "worked like a dog" when he was home. About 5:30 every morning his strong, bellowing voice would announce, "Time to get up!" By six o'clock, if anyone was still in bed, he would shout loudly, "C'mon, Lazy Bones. Are you gonna sleep all day?" They knew the wisest thing to do then was to get up quickly. Everyone had plenty of work to do to provide for the family.

Even though they were struggling themselves, the Millers were quick to help others. Their table could be stretched out with ten additional table leaves, making room for at least 20 people. Annie would supervise as all the children pitched in to help serve guests. Visitors were surprised to find that R. Paul would take time to serve each one personally.

The Millers also spent time with their children, teaching them God's Word and helping them develop a disciplined Christian life. When R. Paul would leave for a speaking engagement, he would give each of his children a verse or passage to learn. The children would work hard to be ready to say the verse to their father when he returned.

Rev. Miller helped develop a Home Mission Board to help the Grace Brethren Fellowship start new churches. He also developed a Board of Evangelism to help the churches reach people who did not know Christ.

R. Paul Miller was continually looking for young people who had an interest in serving the Lord. He would become friends with them and take them with him as he went knocking on doors to tell people about Jesus. He wanted others to catch the joy of witnessing. Wherever he went, whatever he did, it was clear that his passion was to reach people for Christ.

Questions for Discussion

1. R. Paul Miller had his children memorize Scripture. Can you learn a verse each week for the next month?

2. R. Paul served each of his guests at a meal. Can you think of a Bible passage where Jesus served all the disciples?

3. R. Paul traveled around, preaching the gospel. What biblical character is he like? What does "evangelist" mean? What is the "Good News"?

W. A. and Frances Ogden

W. A. and Frances Ogden
1897–1972, 1901–1999

W. A. and Frances Ogden

Genuine

Therefore, my dear brothers, stand firm. Let nothing move you. Always give yourselves fully to the work of the Lord, because you know that your labor in the Lord is not in vain (1 Corinthians 15:58).

Genuine: living an open and proper Christian life

William A. Ogden, a young pastor in his first charge, stood in the church basement, watching the boys scuffle. They all seemed to enjoy the friendly wrestling competition—all except one. Ben, one of the new boys, stood apart from the group, watching the others.

Pastor Ogden walked over and put his hand on Ben's shoulder. "Do you want to join in?" he asked.

Ben hung his head. "I...I don't know how," he said shyly. "All these other guys have dads that wrestle them and teach them the holds. I've never had anyone to wrestle with."

Pastor Ogden nodded thoughtfully. He knew that Ben couldn't even remember his dad. Then he had an idea.

"Why don't you try to take me down, Ben?" he said. Ben looked doubtful.

"Go ahead," Pastor Ogden urged him. "Jump on my back and just see what you can do."

Ben crouched behind the pastor and suddenly jumped on his back. Ben was strong, but he really didn't know what to do next. Pastor Ogden showed him some basic arm and leg holds.

"Now try it," he said encouragingly. Ben was starting to get a feel for what he should do.

The next week Ben asked for more coaching. Soon they were both on the floor trying new holds. The other boys saw them and ran over. "I want to wrestle with the pastor," one of them said. "Me too," said another. Soon Pastor Ogden was letting them all take turns trying to take him down. Out of the corner of his eye, he noticed some boys were challenging Ben. Pastor Ogden smiled to himself as he saw Ben accept the challenge. He knew Ben would soon feel comfortable hanging out with the other boys in the group.

One evening after the Ogdens got home from church, Frances Ogden said, "Honey, can we talk about something?"

Pastor William Augustus Ogden appreciated his wife Frances. She loved to help people, and he trusted her judgment. She seemed always to know just what to do, in any situation. Everyone who knew her saw that she was more interested in others than in herself.

W. A. smiled at her. "What do you want to talk about, Dear?"

"Well, I've noticed that you've been wrestling with the boys at church. Do you really think you should be doing that?" She wrinkled her nose. "It seems terribly undignified."

W. A. frowned thoughtfully. She had a point. In those days church members expected their pastor to be formal and dignified. They certainly wouldn't understand if they saw their pastor involved in horseplay with the boys.

"I guess you're right, Dear," he said. "But I do want the boys to have fun. I guess sometimes I just get carried away. I'll try to be careful."

"Of course, Honey." Frances smiled at her husband. "We wouldn't want anyone to get hurt."

W. A. Ogden was born and raised in the countryside of Iowa. The seventh of 14 children, he went through the eighth grade at the local school in Udell. He played on the Unionville High School basketball team, and even though they had only six players, they won the local championship. "Gusty" also worked on his parents' farm and attended the church his father pastored.

Though he didn't go to college or seminary, and stopped short of graduating from high school, W. A. tried to learn as much as he could. He read whatever books he could find. He especially enjoyed *Pilgrim's Progress* and read it many times. His only other formal training was one year at the Bible Institute of Los Angeles.

When he was 21, the people of his church asked him to serve as an elder. They respected him for his honesty, diligence, and leadership.

But W. A. did not want to be an elder. Instead, he moved to Whittier, California, to live with his aunt. There he started attending the Whittier Brethren Church. That was where he met Frances. She was finishing college at BIOLA and planned to get a nursing degree. She was also a skilled vocal and keyboard musician, a great student of the Bible, and loved to teach and encourage young people and counsel with pastors' wives.

W. A. and Frances were married in 1924. They settled in Iowa for two years, operating a small grocery store. Then they moved back to Fullerton, where W. A. had a job delivering ice. In the days before electric refrigerators, people would buy large blocks of ice to put in iceboxes to keep their food cold.

During this time, though, churches kept asking him to preach. In 1926 W. A. was asked to become pastor of the First Brethren Church in Fillmore, California. So he became Pastor Ogden. He eventually served in several churches in California, Pennsylvania, and Washington, D.C.

W. A. and Frances had many other things going on in their lives, in addition to the responsibilities of the church. They had two girls and three boys whom they taught to love and serve God. During the Great Depression, the children remember their father coming home with treats for them from the grocery store where he worked part-time. He was good in the kitchen, and made wonderful, fluffy pancakes, which he often shaped to look like rabbits or cats. He helped his son Russell design kites that won several contests.

Pastor Ogden was respected by his fellow pastors for his integrity, faithfulness, and commitment to God's Word. He served on the board of Grace College and Seminary, part of that time as its chairman. In appreciation for his outstanding service to the schools and to the Fellowship of Grace Brethren Churches, the board voted to give him an honorary Doctor of Divinity degree. The boy with an eighth grade education was now "Dr. Ogden"!

When Dr. Alva J. McClain (see *Heroes, Vol. 1),* the president of Grace College and Seminary, needed time off to write books on theology, Dr. Ogden was asked to become Executive Vice President of the school. He traveled many miles to raise money for the new buildings the growing school needed. His greatest contribution to the school was his commitment to help and encourage students.

Pastor Ogden was also chosen to serve on the board of the Foreign Missionary Society, making decisions that would help missionaries reach people in other countries with the good news of Jesus. He served in that position for 27 years. He was good at listening to people's needs and helping them find solutions for their problems. He took a special interest in Africa, and his trip there while he was on the board was one he remembered among the most important experiences of his life.

The Ogdens offered a temporary home and family atmosphere to many college students, missionary children, relatives and a retired missionary widow over the years. There was almost always some non-family member living with them. Frances also served as president of WMC, the national women's ministry, for a number of years.

After retirement, the Ogdens lived in Winona Lake, Indiana. They continued to open their home to anyone who needed a meal or a place to stay. Dr. Ogden loved working outdoors in his vegetable garden, and often made his fluffy pancakes.

One day, as winter approached, Dr. Ogden spent the day cleaning out the dead remains of his garden. When he went back inside, he thoughtfully looked out the window. "I don't know what I'm going to do during the long winter months," he told Frances.

That evening he made pancakes for their supper. After they ate, he told Frances that he didn't feel well enough to help with the dishes and stretched out on the couch. A few minutes later he suffered a cerebral hemorrhage and passed into heaven.

Frances lived for 26 more years after her husband died. Someone had introduced her to "pretzel pillows" stuffed with peanut butter. She kept them on hand to offer to guests in her Grace Village apartment.

In 1999 she had a stroke that limited her ability to speak. One day, enjoying a group of visitors by her bed, she signaled for a pen and paper and she wrote, "Jeane, pass the pretzels." She still had her sense of humor.

When her children and grandchildren realized she had only a short time to live, they gathered around her to sing. As they sang an old hymn, "The Way of the Cross Leads Home," she left this world and went home. Her son Russ writes, "Her last breath came as we started the last verse:"

> "Then I bid farewell to the way of the world,
> To walk in it nevermore.
> For my Lord says 'Come,' and I seek my home
> Where He waits at the open door."

"So we sang that verse again, as our last goodbye."

Questions for Discussion

1. When Frances had a concern, she shared it with her husband in a loving way. Part of being genuine is learning how to speak truthfully and considerately. What are some Scripture verses that tell us that?

2. People trusted W. A. Ogden because he was genuine. How do you feel if people aren't genuine? How can you be more genuine in your relationships?

3. The Ogdens helped missionaries' children by giving them a home away from home while their parents were in other countries. What can you do to encourage and help missionaries and pastors?

Allen Bennett

Allen Bennett
1899–1923

Allen Bennett

Persistent

But whatever was to my profit I now consider loss for the sake of Christ. What is more, I consider everything a loss compared to the surpassing greatness of knowing Christ Jesus my Lord, for whose sake I have lost all things. I consider them rubbish, that I may gain Christ (Philippians 3:7–8).

Persistent: unwavering in reaching a goal

"Do you think he'll make it, doctor?" The nurse was standing by, ready to help, as the doctor examined the boy who had just been brought into the hospital.

"I don't know. He's in pretty bad shape. What happened to him?"

"He was in a car that was hit by a train. The cowcatcher on the locomotive carried him about 800 feet, they told me."

The doctor stood, thinking quietly for a while. Finally he straightened his shoulders. "We should talk to the boy's mother. Where is she?" he asked.

The nurse shook her head. Tears filled her eyes. "His mother died in the accident. His grandfather and aunt were also killed."

The doctor sighed. "It'll take a miracle for him to survive. If he does make it, he will need a lot of care. He'll be badly crippled."

What the doctor didn't know was that Allen Bennett had already experienced several miracles in his young life. First, there were complications when he was born. Somehow, he pulled through. Then other problems developed, and the doctors didn't expect him to live through his first few years. Now, just when it seemed his health was improving, this terrible accident happened.

But God had a plan for Allen Bennett, and he did live. For the next year he was transferred from hospital to hospital, being fitted with metal plates to strengthen different parts of his body so he could move more normally. It was a lonely, hard time for the boy. He filled some of the empty times by writing poetry, a habit that stayed with him the rest of his life.

At one of the hospitals, a nurse showed extra motherly interest in the crippled boy who had lost his own mother. This Christian nurse knew what the boy needed most—Jesus Christ. She explained to Allen that he needed to give his heart and life to Jesus. Slowly, Allen began to understand.

One day as she was talking with him, he said, "I want to give my life to Jesus now." She prayed with him. Years later Allen would remember, "I knew then that I would serve the Lord somehow."

Finally, the day came when Allen could go home. In his heart he was making plans. He would go to the Bible Institute of Los Angeles, and then he would give his life to help the mission work in Africa.

Allen kept his commitment. One day he found himself on the deck of the *Vapeur Thysville*, a French ship that would take him from Belgium to the French Congo in Africa. He had spent six months studying in France. He handled the French language so well that Dr. Florence Gribble (see *Heroes, Vol. 1*), who was also in France, decided Allen was ready to join her husband at the new station in Bassai in the heart of Africa. She had written to her husband: "Allen Bennett is a young Hudson Taylor. He travels third class because there is no fourth; dines on next to nothing, or forgets to dine at all, yet has wonderful provision from the Heavenly Father for every actual need."

Five days later, the ship was going through thick fog. The ship had to blow its foghorn every minute or so to let other ships know where it was, since they couldn't see each other in the fog. Allen went below and fell asleep in spite of the noisy foghorn.

Suddenly, he was awakened by a jolt and a deafening crash. Alarms started going off. He ran up to the deck and saw a surging crowd of passengers. Boatmen were grabbing life preservers. Women were shrieking and weeping. Within a few feet of him was a freighter, scraping along the side of the boat. The freighter had broadsided the *Thysville* and put a hole in it.

Dr. Gribble described the scene in her book, *Stranger than Fiction:* "Everywhere men and women commenced to fall on their faces. Doubtless the boat would sink, they thought, and they must make their peace with God while there was yet time. The missionaries went around speaking to those who were imploring God" (p. 150).

A short time afterward the captain announced that the ship was not in danger of sinking. Dr. Gribble noted sadly that most of the passengers stopped praying and went back to their smoking, drinking and gambling. The ship continued on its way to Africa.

Allen was fascinated with Africa from the moment he sighted land. Every day he had lessons in Sango, the central African trade language. Seaports where they stopped along the Congo river showed the influence of various cultures. Colorful hats with large feathers, turbans, painted faces, used and unmatched clothing, filed teeth, and haughty black eyes gave Allen an opportunity to begin adjusting to the new life ahead of him.

Every surface in Africa moved with life. Elephants occasionally swam across the river ahead of them. Large swarms of yellow butterflies often covered the surface of the river. Water snakes disturbed by the passing of the boat swam to the riverbank for safety. Above the constant noise of the boat engines they often heard the chatter of monkeys climbing from tree to tree. Delightfully colored birds flew over them. They even saw a huge crocodile sunning himself on the bank close to their riverboat.

Beautiful Africa held more challenges for Allen. His health problems worsened as they approached the equator. The hot sun, the heavy humidity, and the smell of tropical vegetation made him weak and feverish. He realized more and more his dependence on the Lord. He wrote, "Came down with fever last night. Praise God for the fellowship of His suffering...spent another day in bed...surely the power of Satan is in this land...It has been very warm. Dr. Gribble has not been very well. We are making very poor time."

Allen's health did not improve. As their little boat neared Impfondo, Dr. Gribble said, "Mr. Bennett, I firmly believe we should get you off this boat into better conditions so you can get better. I'll speak to the captain immediately!"

The boat captain pulled to shore to let Allen, Dr. Gribble, and Miss Bonar get off. After four days at Impfondo, Allen was feeling better. He wrote in his diary, "Another day has dragged slowly by. We studied French and Sango again. Tonight we went for a walk. Late into the night I sat on the porch or stood on the riverbank thinking of all that is past. Why is it that I bear the name of Christ, yet am so unlovely? Will there always be unloveliness about me?"

The next day the *Zinga* picked them up to continue their trip. Finally they reached the place where a train could take them to Bangui, the main city in central Africa. At Bangui they met James Gribble (see *Heroes, Vol. 1*). It was time to begin walking the 270 miles from Bangui to Bassai.

Almost 100 people traveled together—over mud, rocks, and tree roots, through heavily wooded areas, under the hot tropical sun. When they came to a river, they had to wade through it or cross on logs that had fallen across it. Allen and the Gribbles struggled along, although all three were sick.

The first day they traveled only five miles. Allen wrote in his diary, "By the light of a smoky lantern in a rest house eight kilometers after leaving Bangui, I am writing these words. Surrounded by trunks, head aching, tired, and weary in body, we are still in peace. This is my first experience on safari...I rode in the tepois (padded seat mounted on two poles, carried by four porters). It is a weird and wonderful experience."

Along the way, Allen wrote this poem:

Going On With Jesus

"Going on with Jesus, in the blessed sunlit way,
Walking closely by His side, rejoicing day by day,
Trusting in His kindly care and resting in His love,
Always pressing onward to that resting place above.

"Going on with Jesus, resting always on His arm,
Comforted in sorrow, kept from every harm,
Storm clouds gather 'round about and settle o'er the way;
Jesus speaks in accents low, and rolls the clouds away.

"Going on with Jesus, up the rugged mountain side,
Rough and hard the pathway, where deceiving dangers hide.
Walking with the Savior, up the wind-swept, winding trail,
In His peace abiding midst the fiercest storm and gale.

"Going on with Jesus, in the sunset's after glow,
Down beside the seashore where the currents ebb and flow.
Days of toil and trouble, by His grace, will soon be past,
Going on with Jesus through the pearly gates at last."

Allen Lee Bennett 1922

Allen still had fevers from time to time, but as his strength returned he was eager to continue. At times he felt well enough to ride his iron horse (bicycle), which the Gribbles had given him. One of the last pictures taken of Allen was of him carrying his bicycle across a river, walking on a large tree that had fallen across the stream.

On January 9, 1923, he wrote in his diary, "Good night. Temperature normal in morning. Left Baumana and rode the iron horse to Gazeli. Just made it. Temperature 99°. Went to bed again. Don't feel very well."

Allen never wrote in his diary again. The Gribbles took care of him in a little mud hut. On January 17 they realized Allen was getting worse. He didn't speak much, but he said, "There is nothing between my Lord and me." Shortly before midnight they heard him say the word *better*. A few minutes later the Lord took him "through the pearly gates at last." He had been traveling two and a half months since leaving Belgium.

The Gribbles lovingly buried him. They were still 90 miles from the mission station at Bassai.

The Gribbles were terribly disappointed to lose such a promising worker. When word of Allen Bennett's death reached the churches in the United States, however, many young people stepped forward, volunteering to take Allen's place on the mission field. The Lord knew this was better.

God did not overlook the sacrifice of His servants. That part of central Africa is now one of the most evangelized areas of the world.

Questions for Discussion

1. Allen accepted Jesus as his Savior because a nurse told him about Jesus. Do you know someone you can tell about Jesus?

2. Allen praised God even when he was sick. Why did he? Could you?

3. Allen was persistent in his desire to share Christ. Why are we afraid to share Christ? How can we be more like Allen?

Orville Jobson

Orville Jobson
1900–1974

Orville Jobson

Dedication

No one who puts his hand to the plow and looks back is fit for service in the kingdom of God (Luke 9:62).

Dedication: faithful determination to do what is right

Orville Jobson's push-car raced through the African jungle heat. It had a single motorcycle wheel with a chair-like frame mounted on it. Two poles in front allowed a person standing between the poles to guide it, while two people behind it pushed on a railing behind the chair.

Because the tropical weather was so hard on their health, missionaries often had to have some sort of transportation to get them to their destination. In addition, it gave them a wonderful opportunity to get to know the people transporting them.

Orville was on a 270-mile trip to join missionary James Gribble (see *Heroes, Vol. 1*) at the mission station in the village of Bassai in the Oubangui-Chari province of central Africa. Suddenly he stopped his push-car. All along the rough, winding path in front of him were strewn pieces of a tepois!

His heart sank. He recognized the fabric from that tepois. A tepois was a fabric seat hung over long poles so someone could sit in it while strong men carried them. Orville had watched his traveling companions, two lady missionaries, leave in that very tepois the night before.

The African heat had been very hard on Miss Myers and Miss Hillegas, and they had begged to be allowed to travel during the cooler night hours. Reluctantly, he had agreed to the plan. Some of the 100 porters they had hired to help them get their equipment to Bassai had gone with the ladies, and the rest would travel with Orville the next day, bringing most of the baggage.

Now it looked as though that decision had been a mistake. Here was the broken tepois, and there was no sign of the ladies or the porters. Could wild animals have done this? Or was it warriors from the local tribes? There were cannibals in the area—people who ate the flesh of their human enemies.

Orville knew that the French government had not wanted foreigners to go to central Africa because the tribes in the area were so dangerous. James Gribble and the other missionaries had spent three years trying to convince the French government to let them enter the area. Now it looked like the French government was right. What a way to begin his missionary career!

Orville knew that Satan did not want missionaries to go into the heart of Africa to tell the people there about Jesus. He also knew there was only one way to defeat Satan's efforts to keep missionaries out. Orville Jobson prayed under his breath as he hurried on with his porters. He must trust God to take care of the lady missionaries.

He encouraged his porters to hurry. As they continued the journey, they kept alert for the travelers, or for signs of a struggle. There was no sign of his friends! What could have happened to them? Once again, Orville lifted his heart in prayer to his Lord.

Finally, as it began to get dark, they saw the village where they were to stop. Everything seemed calm. Orville held his breath as he entered the village. In the growing darkness he suddenly saw a white face—then another. The ladies were safe! They explained to their relieved friend that their tepois had broken. Their porters had found other poles and stretched blankets between them to make seats for the ladies.

Orville Jobson learned an important lesson in faith and trust that day. He would learn many more in his 36 years of serving God in Africa. Eventually, the Central African Republic would become one of the most evangelized countries in the world.

Two years earlier, Orville Jobson had been studying at the Philadelphia School of the Bible. Dr. Alva J. McClain (see *Heroes, Vol. 1)*, pastor of the First Brethren Church of Philadelphia, was one of his teachers. Dr. McClain kept telling his classes about the need to share the good news of Jesus with people in other countries. Immediately Orville was interested. A year later, when the missionary board decided to send someone to help pioneer missionary James Gribble, Orville applied and was accepted September 3, 1921.

Dr. McClain later wrote,

"That left but two months in which to purchase and assemble his outfit. And according to the Constitution of the African Mission, none of the General Funds can be used for personal outfit! The money must come in gifts designated specially for that purpose. Brother Jobson had no time to go about in the churches to inform the people of his life work because the Board asked him to devote his entire time to study French until he sailed. So we held some prayer meetings in which we definitely laid the matter before God.

"I can remember now that someone in my Men's Bible Class asked how much money we ought to pray for. I answered, 'He must have $400, and he could use $800.' Well, God answered our prayers. During those last two months, money came from all directions. On the morning of our farewell services for Brother Jobson, he told me I could announce that his outfit fund had reached $801.01! The $1.01 was given in pennies by Brother Huette's little boy at Dayton in order that 'the little black boys might hear about Jesus!'"

By the end of the following Sunday the outfit fund for Mr. Jobson had reached $900. Once again, God had answered prayer.

Meanwhile, Miss Charlotte Hillegas had also heard about the need for someone to tell the African people about God. She went to France to study French, the government language of that part of Africa. She also spent two months in London, England, studying tropical medicine so she would know how to deal with diseases that were common in the hot climate near the equator. She was to be a companion to Miss Estella Myers, who had gone to Africa with the Gribbles.

On December 31, 1921, Miss Myers, Miss Hillegas, and Mr. Jobson arrived at the new Bassai mission station. Orville was amazed at what Mr. Gribble had done to establish the station. He was building homes for them—six-sided homes that he designed and laid out using only a pocket compass, an inverted aluminum cup, an empty oatmeal tin, a table, and a pair of opera glasses (binoculars) with a rope for his measuring line. In addition to these primitive planning instruments, one of the buildings was along the edge of a sharp cliff, and the workers were native assistants who had no idea what Mr. Gribble was trying to do!

About a year after arriving in Africa, Mr. Jobson and Miss Hillegas were married. Shortly after that, James Gribble died. Orville Jobson was left with the responsibility to carry on the work.

Sometimes, when Americans go to another country to reach the people, they feel that it's faster to set everything up for the people—providing the finances and planning for their church building, for example. However, the Lord had led James Gribble to write down specific plans for how the mission would do its work of bringing people to Christ. He was convinced that the Africans themselves should be trained in the Word and go out to reach their own people. He also believed the African churches that developed should make their own decisions, instead of being instructed by the missionaries.

The small group of missionaries with Orville Jobson worked out plans that would allow the Africans to take responsibility for reaching their own people. One of his goals was to inspire and prepare the African people to reach unreached tribes and villages. He carefully chose young Africans and taught them the Word so they could help others. These young men became very capable pastors, and helped the African churches establish their own independence while still working well with the mission and the missionaries.

Orville Jobson was appointed field superintendent to oversee all the mission stations in Africa in 1939. He served in that position for more than 23 years. In 1947 he was awarded an honorary Doctor of Divinity degree from Grace Theological Seminary, and many people remember him as "Dr. Jobson." Ten years later, he gave a series of messages at Grace Theological Seminary describing the wonderful history of the mission work in Central Africa. Those messages were the basis of a book that was later published, *Conquering Oubangui-Chari for Christ.*

Throughout his life, Orville Jobson never lost his love for Christ and for the African people. Even after he and Charlotte retired, they agreed to go back to Africa to help take care of needs there.

Questions for Discussion

1. When Orville was afraid for the ladies' safety, he prayed. How important is prayer in our lives? Should we pray only when in trouble?

2. Orville asked for money to help him go to Africa. People prayed, and the money came in. Have you had prayers answered? Do you know of any missionaries who need money you could give?

3. Mr. Gribble built homes for the missionaries in Africa, even though he was not an architect. Can you think of a Scripture verse that reminds us that God can help us in every situation?

Charles W. Mayes

Charles W. Mayes
1901–1979

Charles W. Mayes

Preparing Leaders

And the things you have heard me say in the presence of many witnesses entrust to reliable men who will also be qualified to teach others (2 Timothy 2:2).

Preparing leaders: training and preparing the way for those who will lead the way in the future

Twelve-year-old Charles finished refilling the water dish for the chickens. He squinted his eyes toward the sun, measuring how low it was in the sky. "It's almost milking time," he sighed. He still needed to throw down feed for the cows. He'd have to hurry.

Charles headed toward the silo, the tall, round building next to the barn. He opened the door and climbed the wooden ladder to where the feed was stored. At the top, he reached for the pitchfork to start throwing down the feed.

Suddenly, Charles stopped. He stood up straight. The pitchfork clanged from his hand onto the floor.

"That's it!" he exclaimed. "I have to do it myself!"

Charles had been thinking all day about what he had heard the night before. The church was having revival services, a special time when they brought in an evangelist to tell people how they could be saved. The evangelist had stressed Matthew 18:3: "Unless you change and become like little children, you will never enter the kingdom of heaven." Then he had said, "No one can do it for you."

At first, it hadn't made sense to Charles. His parents were good Christians, and he had always assumed that meant he was a Christian, too. After all, he had always gone to church, and he had never doubted that God existed or that the Bible was true.

But he had just been hit by a new understanding of what it meant to be a Christian. "He meant that I have to make a decision whether I will follow Christ. My parents can't make me a Christian—I have to choose for myself!"

Charles fell to his knees there in the silo. He took off his cap, out of reverence for God. Then he prayed, "Lord, if you will allow me to be at the meeting tomorrow night, I will go forward at the invitation and give my heart to God. I'll even become a preacher if you want me to."

He did not know what else to say, but he meant what he said and felt relieved that he had told the Lord what he felt in his heart.

He finished feeding the animals and went in to tell his family about his prayer. They were glad to hear it, because they had been praying he would make a decision for Christ. Later he loved to tell this story whenever he had a chance to give his testimony.

At that time, it was hard for anyone to imagine Charles W. Mayes becoming a preacher. He was a quiet, timid country boy. His only public activity was playing trombone in the school band. He enjoyed playing trombone and could even play the difficult trumpet parts on it.

When Charles graduated from high school he studied at the business college and the conservatory of music in Oberlin, near his hometown of Sullivan, Ohio. After that training he went to Ashland College. There he was asked to become the leader of the college's first band. He also began traveling with a gospel team, where he would sing and play his trombone.

As leader of the ministry band, Charles was getting used to dealing with the unexpected. Still, it was a surprise one night when he was told that the evangelist was sick, and he would

need to preach. Charles immediately began trying to find someone else to preach. Finally, he realized he had no choice. He
would have to preach.

After that night, Charles was on his way to becoming a
preacher. He got a job teaching in a one-room school. He taught
first through eighth grade—all at once! But people kept asking
him to come preach at their churches, and his interest in minis-
tering to people kept growing. He became convinced that God
was definitely calling him to preach.

He married Marjorie Stone and went to pastor his first church
in Lanark, Illinois. Later he pastored in Des Moines, Iowa, and
in Whittier, California. These experiences prepared him for his
next assignment.

In 1936 he was asked to help publish *The Brethren Evangelist,* a magazine for Brethren churches. At that time there was a
lot of confusion and tension in the church. Some Brethren people were saying that the Bible was out-of-date. When Charles
became editor of the *Evangelist,* he was careful to include
articles that defended the belief that the Bible was God's Word
and should not be treated like just another book. Because of his
stand, a number of leaders in the national church decided he
should be removed from his job as editor.

One day a large group of men came into Charles' office.
They told him they needed to use his office for a meeting, and
asked him to leave. Charles said, "No, I have work to do. Go
right ahead with your meeting. I won't bother you."

The men again asked him to leave his own office. Charles
explained, "No. This is work that must be finished." Finally, the
men left.

The next day a constable came to Charles' office and told
him to leave. Charles realized that he must obey the public of-
ficial and leave. "All right," he said. "Just let me get my things
first."

"Sorry," the constable told him. "You must leave right this
minute."

Charles left. He went down to the police station. Soon he
was back with a police escort. He was able to get his belong-

ings and personal documents. Later, those materials would be very useful as Charles helped start the new Brethren Missionary Herald Company, the publishing arm of the Fellowship of Grace Brethren Churches.

In 1943 Charles Mayes was asked to go to South Pasadena, California, to pioneer a church in that area. Three years later he was asked to take Dr. L. S. Bauman's place (see pp. 11–15) as pastor of the large First Brethren Church in Long Beach. Charles served there for 22 years. He also taught classes at the Bible Institute of Los Angeles, where he received a Doctor of Divinity degree.

Charles had two great dreams in his life. One was to make sure that Christian publications were available. While in California, he bought a printing press and began printing the church bulletin. Soon he was printing bulletins for other churches. Then he started printing teaching materials, also. He taught his sons and other people to run the press, and soon they could take over the printing.

Pastor Mayes' other dream was that Christian families would have a way to give their children a truly Christian education. The Bible, prayer, and the mention of God were gradually being squeezed out of public education. Charles Mayes realized that a student is not fully educated unless he knows God's truth. He spoke with other pastors in the area, and in 1947 Brethren Church School opened with 102 students. It continued to add at least one grade each year until it contained all elementary and high school grades and covered two campuses.

Pastor Mayes was very involved in seeing that the school would fulfill its mission to young hearts and minds. He taught in the high school, led the school orchestra in presenting public concerts, showed up to help on work days to fix the facilities, and worked tirelessly behind the scenes providing direction and support. Many people who are working for Christ throughout the world today received their early education at Brethren Church Schools in Long Beach and Paramount, California.

Dr. Charles Mayes was also co-founder of what is now known as the Association of Christian Schools, International (ACSI).

He served long terms on both the Grace Brethren Foreign Missionary Society and the Grace Theological Seminary boards.

Charles was a tender-hearted man whose tears came easily. He had a great sense of humor and a sparkling wit. His life was bathed in prayer and ministry. Near the end of his life he discovered he had cancer. After an extended time of pain and suffering, he and Marjorie realized that the time for his homegoing was near. They prayed all one night, telling the Lord that he was ready to go. The next day the Lord took him home to heaven. He was 78 years old.

Questions for Discussion

1. Charles was willing to be used by God. Have you told God you are willing to let Him use you also?

2. Even though Charles was afraid to preach, he realized he would have to do it, so he did. Can you remember a time you did something even though you were afraid?

3. Charles believed the Bible was the most important book ever written and that it was God's words to help prepare leaders. How can the Bible be used today to train Christian leaders?

Jake Kliever

Jake Kliever
1905–1989

Jake Kliever

Studious

But grow in the grace and knowledge of our Lord and Savior Jesus Christ. To him be glory both now and forever! Amen (2 Peter 3:18).

Studious: willing to study to find answers for life

"Hey, Goat, that girl's following us again."

The boy who was called Goat turned around. "Oh, no, not that Freda Neufeld again!" he thought to himself. She was such a pest!

"Go home," he shouted to her. "Your mama's looking for you." He already knew, deep inside, that she wouldn't change her mind. She was one of the most determined girls he'd ever met.

"This is a free country," the girl answered. She kept coming.

Suddenly a rock landed on the path in front of her. She drew back for a moment, then started walking again. Another rock landed even closer. She hesitated for a moment, and the boys took advantage of her uncertainty. Another rock hit her leg.

"I'm going to tell my mama on you," she yelled defiantly. "Jake Kliever, she'll tell your mama, and you'll be in trouble."

Another rock whizzed by her; then she turned and ran down the path.

The boys dropped their rocks and turned to continue walking. "You're gonna be in trouble, Goat," one of his friends warned. Jake shrugged. He was used to being in trouble. His mischievous nature could never resist the temptation to play a practical joke, tease someone, or try something he wasn't supposed to do.

Jake's friends called him "Goat" partly because of his white hair, but also because of his endless energy. He was friendly and outgoing, and his friends followed him, a natural leader. He had been born in Canada, but his family had moved a year before to Dallas, Oregon. He had quickly made new friends, but they didn't include Freda Neufeld. Her family had also moved to Dallas from Canada. What a bother that girl was!

Meanwhile, Jake's mother didn't need to know details of what he was doing. She knew quite well his habit of getting into mischief. Jake's mother was praying for him every day. She hoped that someday her son would learn to do what was right.

Jake was a very intelligent boy, and before he grew up he had learned Dutch and German in addition to English. He always wanted to learn something new. At age nine, Jake decided he wanted to become a Christian. But when he talked with the adults in his church, they just patted him on the head and told him to be a good boy.

Finally, when Jake was 18, he heard the simple plan of salvation. Immediately, he knew this was what he had wanted to know. He asked Christ to take over his life.

This event changed Jake's life. He became a constant witness for Jesus. When he had opportunity to travel, he always tried to take a train instead of his car, because it gave him a chance to meet more people and tell them about Christ.

Jake was especially gifted in music. When his family moved to Los Angeles, he had many opportunities to use his talent. He was asked to lead adult, youth, and children's choirs, sing bass in a quartet, and play cello in a string quartet. The University of Southern California asked him to sing in their special "glee club," even though he wasn't a student there!

"Jake," said his mother one day, "I'm going to have a party for people in this area who are also from Oregon. Can you free your schedule to be here?"

Jake was glad to be invited. A number of his old friends were in the area, and it would be good to see them. The day of the party, Jake had a wonderful time.

Suddenly, he noticed a girl sitting on the fence, watching everything that was happening around her with a contented smile.

"Who is that?" he asked his friends.

They looked surprised. "Don't you know her? You should. That's Freda Neufeld. She's just finishing college at the Bible Institute of Los Angeles."

Jake could hardly believe it. "That girl who used to pester us?" he asked in amazement.

Later that afternoon, Jake decided to take some of the guests for a ride in his Model "A" roadster. With a lot of skillful planning, Jake was able to arrange it so Freda "accidentally" ended up sitting next to him. That ride was the start of a romance that would last more than fifty-five years.

Jake really wanted to ask Freda to marry him. But he was also convinced that God was calling him to go to Africa as a missionary. What should he do? He finally decided that if God wasn't calling Freda to Africa, he would have to go alone. It was one of the hardest decisions he had ever made. Finally he got up the nerve to talk to Freda about it. To his surprise, he learned she believed God had been calling *her* to Africa, as well.

The Klievers went to Africa in 1937. They were well-liked by the people, and made many contributions to the needs of the field. Jake had studied Greek and Hebrew, and had also learned French and Sango in addition to the languages he had learned as a boy. His background in languages was very useful when he was asked to help translate the New Testament into Sango, the trade language of the people.

The committee doing the translation had many challenges. For example, both English and the original Greek New Testament use the word "heart" to refer to the center of a person's being. But in Sango, the heart is not recognized as the center. So the translators ended up writing, "Trust in the Lord with all your *liver*."

"Trust in the LORD with all your heart
   and lean not on your own understanding;
in all your ways acknowledge him,
   and he will make your paths straight" (Proverbs 3:5–6).

Jake Kliever was a curious person who always wanted to know as much as possible. When his daughter Donna had malaria, and the usual quinine treatment was no longer helping her, Jake started doing research on malaria. Finally, he learned about a new medication, Antibraun, that would fight the disease without hurting her kidneys. His family remembers him often poring over books to find an answer he needed.

Jake and Freda's motto was, "Dare to find God's will for your life, then make that your BIG business." One day Jake brought up a topic that had been bothering him. "Freda, dear," he said, "What do you think about leaving our girls in the United States the next time we go back for furlough?" Freda didn't answer right away. She, too, had been thinking about that question. "Anne will be thirteen and Donna will be nine. Do you really think we need to leave them there?"

During their yearlong furlough in the United States, Jake and Freda agonized over their decision. Several churches asked him to consider coming to be their pastor.

"If I took one of those pastorates, we could all stay together," Jake said to his family.

"But Daddy," said Anne, "You know the language of those people in Africa. If you don't go back, who will teach them?"

"Well," said Jake, "Maybe we should take you girls back with us so we don't have to be separated."

"But, Daddy, there's no school for me there," said Donna.

So the family kept praying. Then one day Dr. and Mrs. W.A. Ogden (see pp. 35–40) contacted the Klievers. "Our youngest child is grown up and leaving home, and we can't stand the thought of not having children in our home. Would your girls like to come and live with us?"

Jake and Freda knew what their BIG business was, and they also knew their girls needed an education. They accepted the offer, though it was a very hard decision both for them and their daughters. Years later Jake remembered, "Freda and I used to joke about them keeping our tears in a bottle up in heaven." Psalm 56:8 says, "You tell my wanderings; put my tears into your bottle, are they not in your book?" Jake added, "Someday there will be a first-rate bottle-washing in heaven" (paraphrase).

Throughout his life, anytime you couldn't find Jake, you'd be wise to look for a group of children. You would probably find him with them, pulling a quarter out of their ear or swallowing his tongue, using such interesting tricks as a chance to share God's love with them.

As Jake grew older, his eyes started giving him trouble. He used a magnifying page reader to continue studying. He was always preparing another Bible study.

Toward the end of his life, he was on pain medication that caused him to hallucinate. In one of his last days on earth, those around him heard him speaking in Sango, telling someone where to put the boxes and books. Africa was still on his mind and heart.

Before that, when he had realized that he didn't have long on this earth, Jake wanted to share his testimony. Confidently he declared, "If I had my life to live over, I'd do the same things." Jake had joyfully done whatever God had told him to do, and he was rejoicing at the hope of seeing his Savior.

Questions for Discussion

1. Jake used his education and languages to help the people in Africa. How might you use what you study to help others?

2. Before Jake died, he said if he could live over again, he would do the same things. In other words, he had no regrets about his life. Can you think of a biblical character who lived with no regrets?

3. Although Jake loved Freda, he knew he had to do what God
   wanted him to do. Can you think of a time when you've had
   to choose God's will over your own?

Noel Gaiwaka

Noel Gaiwaka
1910–1996

Noel Gaiwaka

Faithful to the End

He who goes out weeping, carrying seed to sow, will return with songs of joy, carrying sheaves with him (Psalm 126:6).

Faithful: dependable in both good and bad times

Eleven-year-old Noel Gaiwaka stared from behind a bush at the strange creature coming down the trail. The creature was moving toward Noel's new home. Noel wasn't sure whether to laugh—or run away.

This was certainly the most incredible animal the young African had ever seen. The creature had no mouth or tail. It consisted entirely of long, thin bones with bundles strapped to them. Something was on its back—something with a face like a man's, but without any color. Two hands, also colorless, were grasping the long, bony ears of the creature. On the rider's head was something that looked like the shell of a giant egg. The rider was moving his knees up and down as he rode. The creature carrying him ran on two large, round legs that turned as it bumped along the trail.

"Iron Horse," Noel whispered under his breath. There was no need to run away. His cousin had told him about the iron horse. That pale rider must be the white man who was trying to learn the Karre language. Noel's cousin had been chosen to help teach him the native language of the area.

Noel had been living with his cousin only a short time. When he was born, his father had leprosy, a serious illness that deformed his body and caused people to be afraid of catching his disease. Noel's mother had belonged to another tribe, so Noel was not well accepted by the other people of his community. After his parents died, Noel's cousin in Bassai had agreed to take care of him.

That evening the white man called the people of the village together. Although he was struggling with the difficult Karre language, it was obvious that he wanted very much to tell them something. He began to talk about his God, a very different God from the spirits Noel's people feared. This God loved people and wanted to help them. He had even sent His Son to die so they could escape punishment for their sins.

Noel sat listening, hesitant one minute and eager the next. Why should he care about the white man's God? From everything he knew of white men, they were only interested in having people work for them to make their own lives easier. But his heart told him that he should at least investigate what this white man was saying. What if there really was a God who cared about him and could help remove all the guilt from his heart?

Every evening the missionary, James Gribble (see *Heroes, Vol. 1),* would call the people together. Noel would listen carefully to what he said. As time passed, he began to know in his heart that what this man was saying was true. Joyfully, he committed his life to the one true God. Noel had the privilege of being one of the first seven believers baptized in that part of Africa.

Noel was very bright and worked hard. One day the Bassai chief stopped to talk to him. The chief wanted to be a part of a small clothes-making business, and he had bought a sewing machine. He promised Noel a great future if he would learn to sew.

Noel was intrigued. This was an interesting machine. You could take two pieces of fabric, hold them together, and push them through the machine. Once they had gone through the machine, they were fastened together. Noel was a quick learner, and soon was sewing well.

But Noel had another desire burning deep in his heart. He had given his life to the one true God. He had helped teach about God in the surrounding villages, and it brought him great joy to help people know this wonderful God he loved so much. He knew he had to decide how he would use his time. The more he prayed, the more Noel was convinced that if he kept the sewing machine, he would miss his opportunity to spread the good news about Jesus to his people. Bravely, he returned the sewing machine to the tribal chief and asked him to find someone else to take advantage of the opportunity.

When Noel was 17, a mission school opened. Noel was one of the first students to attend. He learned more about the Bible, and also learned to speak French. He worked hard, and soon he was asked to preach and teach God's Word to others. He knew for sure now that this was his ministry for life.

Soon he was asked to go to Bozoum to help teach a small group of believers there. Two years later he was asked to return to Bassai—as the pastor of the church there. Now he could be with his own tribe again, where he was comfortable with the customs, language, and country. Five years later he married Esther, who would be his partner for more than 50 years.

After Noel had been back at Bassai for about 17 years, Dr. Orville Jobson (see pp. 51–55), his French Bible teacher, asked Noel to go with him to the national capital city, Bangui. The first Sunday they had 300 people show up for the services in Sango, the trade language of the area, and 35 for the service in French. Noel had been busy inviting his countrymen to hear the message of Jesus.

A year later, about 1,200 people were coming to the services where Noel Gaiwaka preached. Over the next 35 years, 33 churches were planted by Pastor Noel, members of his church, and the nearby missionaries. The Jobsons and other missionaries exclaimed, "This is the Lord's doing; it is marvelous in our eyes" (Psalm 118:23, NASB).

As Noel continued to show his people how a Christian should live, the people began calling him Koko Noel, a special term showing love and respect. Both his people and the missionaries trusted him, and he was a great help to the missionaries when they did not fully understand the ways and attitudes of the African people. In 1960 he was recognized by the government of the Central African Republic for his outstanding work—they awarded him the "Chevalier (Knight) of Merit" award.

In 1969 Brethren missionary Wayne Beaver was asked to serve as the director of a great evangelism program sponsored by the Brethren and Baptist missions. Pastor Noel was enthusiastic about reaching the capital city of Bangui where he was pastor. He trained leaders, organized prayer meetings, and preached day after day. About 50 more churches were established as a result of this effort to reach the capital.

Noel Gaiwaka was a wise leader for the Grace Brethren churches in Africa. He and Pastor Marc Voloungou led them to adopt a church constitution, which helped prevent a few people from taking power and dictating to all the churches. He also helped stabilize the churches during hard times when the country was going through wars and revolutions. In 1971 he traveled to the United States to represent the African believers at the national conference of the Fellowship of Grace Brethren Churches. In 1987 CE National recognized his years of faithfully reaching his own countrymen by giving him the Evangelist of the Year award.

Pastor Noel began to lose his eyesight and his hearing, and had to retire after 55 years as a pastor. But up until his death in 1996, pastors from all over would come to see him and hear his advice for their ministries.

Dr. Wayne Beaver, who worked closely with Noel, remembers the last time he saw him: "In his final years when he became increasingly immobilized, he was lovingly cared for by his daughter in Bangui. On my last visit to Bangui, he had not responded to anyone for some time. He was blind and deaf. As I greeted him, his son-in-law yelled in his ear, 'Dr. Beaver is here.' He became greatly agitated and grabbed my hand and held on to it for some time. His memory was still good!"

Questions for Discussion

1. Noel Gaiwaka was faithful in reaching out to his own people, and he was rewarded for it with the "Chevalier of Merit" award. How will we be rewarded in heaven?

2. Noel was called "Koko Noel" after he had been preaching for a long time. This name was special. What are some names we call Jesus to give Him love and respect?

3. Noel traveled to the U.S. to represent African believers. We represent Christ to the world. Can you think of Scripture verses that tell us how to do this?

Ralph Colburn

Ralph Colburn
1916–1996

Ralph Colburn

Serving

I consider my life worth nothing to me, if only I may finish the race and complete the task the Lord Jesus has given me—the task of testifying to the gospel of God's grace (Acts 20:24).

Serving: joyfully helping anyone in need

Mark stood on the sidewalk in Fort Lauderdale, Florida, as the parade moved past him. There were floats, clowns, and cars with big painted banners. But the part Mark liked best were the kids, some of them his own age, on decorated bicycles.

"What does that sign say?" Mark's little brother Tom was asking.

Mark kept his eyes on his friend Dan, who was riding in the middle of the parade. Dan had taken his hands off the handlebars. "Why is Dan in a parade?" Mark wondered.

"Mark!" Tom insisted. "What does it say?"

Mark forced his eyes to go to the big car Tom was pointing at. He read out loud, "Come to Sunday School."

"What's Sunday School?" Tom asked. Mark shook his head. "I'm not sure. It must be fun, though."

Later that afternoon Mark and Tom were playing marbles in the front yard when Mark saw Dan ride by. He called out to him. Dan spun his bike around and turned into the driveway. "What was that parade about?" Mark asked.

"Oh, that's to get people to come to our church. Do you want to come tomorrow?"

"I do!" Tom yelled. "I want to come. Will you go with me, Mark?"

So the next morning the two boys walked two blocks down the street to the church. It hadn't been easy to get permission from their parents. Finally their mom told their dad, "I know we don't need religion, dear, but it won't hurt the boys to go with their friend."

Mark and Tom enjoyed Sunday School. Soon they were going every week. Dan made sure they met the pastor, a man who always seemed excited. Pastor Ralph Colburn liked kids; they could tell that right away.

One day as they were leaving church, Mark saw his mother standing at the door, talking to Pastor Colburn. "What is Mom doing here?" he wondered. On the way home she explained, "The church always sends us bulletins, and when I looked at one this morning I saw that the message was on 'What are the good things of Heaven?' I was curious, so I came. I can't wait to tell your father what I heard."

The next week the entire family went to church. Soon they accepted Christ as their Savior. Life was changing fast in Mark and Tom's home.

One day Pastor Colburn announced there would be another parade to invite people to Sunday School. "Do you think we can get 600 people to come?" Pastor Colburn asked the congregation. "If we do, that will break our record attendance. So, if we do, I will let you break a phonograph record over my head."

After church, Pastor Colburn stopped Mark at the door. "Will you be riding your bike in the parade?" he asked. "I see you ride by my house a lot."

Mark's dad laughed. "You're right," he said. "Mark rides his bike all the time. He's going to wear it out if he doesn't give it a break."

"I'd rather see a bike wear out from a boy riding it than rust because no one uses it," Pastor Colburn laughed. "We'll see you in the parade."

The next Sunday there were more than 600 people in church. Someone said, "Are they really going to break a phonograph record over the pastor's head?" Some of the adults laughed. "No, I'm guessing the pastor will find a way to back out of the deal," one said.

But when Pastor Colburn got up to speak, he said, "Where's that phonograph record? I'm ready." Then he sat in the "seat of honor" while they broke the record over his head. Everyone was smiling and laughing. As Mark watched, he thought, "The one who has the biggest smile is Pastor Colburn himself."

Ralph Colburn was seven years old when his family moved from Wheatland, North Dakota, to Pomona, California. Five years later, on March 28, 1928, he accepted Jesus as his Savior while attending a boys and girls Bible class after school. He always remembered that date as his spiritual birthday.

A year later his family moved to Long Beach, California, and visited the "Fifth and Cherry" Brethren Church. Everyone called the church that because it had been built at the corner where Fifth Street met Cherry Street. Young Ralph quickly got involved in volunteering at the church however he could. He taught a class of young boys, sang in a quartet, and went out with the gospel team to tell others about Christ. He went to the Bible Institute of Los Angeles (BIOLA), and after graduating from there, started taking classes at Westmont College.

About that time, his father died. Ralph had to take over the family business to support himself and his mother. Still, he didn't let it keep him from serving the Lord. He started a branch church nearby, and also started a high school youth group, where he soon had 50 students coming. Forty of those students accepted Christ as their Savior.

Ralph Colburn's interest in helping young people was soon noticed by other church leaders, and in January of 1948 he was asked to become the first National Youth Director for the Brethren Church. He served in that position for six years, helping churches learn how to train their young people.

Ralph also had a special love interest during this time. While he was in college, he had met Julia Rowland and they had become very good friends. After 10 years of courtship, Ralph asked Julia to marry him. He was delighted when she said "yes."

The next Sunday Ralph's pastor, Glen O'Neal, announced their engagement in the morning church service. The congregation sat for a second in stunned silence. Then someone shouted, "Amen!" Everyone began clapping enthusiastically for the new couple.

Ralph and Julia believed God wanted them to start a church in Fort Lauderdale, Florida, so six months later they moved there. They were convinced that if they could reach the children in the area, they would reach their families too. Ralph had worked with young people enough to know that they need plenty of activities and challenges to keep them involved.

So they focused on getting the message of Jesus to as many people as possible. They trained teachers and brought in representatives from publishing houses to show their teaching materials and give new ideas. They invited visiting missionaries to tell the kids about what they were doing in their country. They sponsored contests for inviting friends and learning Bible verses. Like Mark and Tom, many children and their families came to Christ through the ministry of the Colburns.

Pastor Ralph was 80 years old when he became very sick and doctors told him he would probably die. He made a videotape to show to his friends at his funeral. In the video he said, "I can still say, 'This is the day the Lord has made; I *will* rejoice and be glad in it.' God has given me something glad, something happy, about each day, even when I'm feeling miserable physically."

He ended his tape by saying, "And why fear? Something that God has prepared—you *know*—has to be better than anything here."

Questions for Discussion

1. Ralph Colburn always remembered his spiritual birthday. Do you have a spiritual birthday?

2. Pastor Colburn kept his promise to let the phonograph record be broken over his head. How important is it to keep promises? What has Jesus promised us?

3. Pastor Colburn served others. What did Jesus say about serving?

Evelyn Fuqua

Evelyn Fuqua
(1917–1979)

Evelyn Fuqua

Compassion

But when he saw the multitudes, he was moved with compassion on them, because they fainted, and were scattered abroad, as sheep having no shepherd (Matthew 9:36, KJV).

Compassion: caring about the needs of others

The barrel of the gun was pointed right at him, but the man didn't see it. He was enjoying his walk along the mountain trail. The young people he had brought with him from his church were getting farther and farther behind. They weren't nearly as interested in the scenery as they were in talking with Miss Evelyn, the young missionary who operated the mission station they had come to help. The young people were full of questions, and Miss Evelyn patiently answered each one.

They had just arrived at the station after a long trip, and they were glad when Miss Evelyn offered to show them around. It felt good to stretch their legs and breathe the mountain air. They had come to help with cleanup and repairs at the small mission station of Dryhill, Kentucky, high in the Appalachian mountains.

The man looked up curiously at the small cabin perched on the side of the mountain above him. It looked like an interesting place to visit. He turned to go up the steep path leading to the cabin.

Suddenly he felt a sharp tap on his shoulder. "Please wait right where you are, Pastor," he heard Miss Evelyn say. Then he heard her call up to the cabin, "Good morning, Luke. This is Miss Evelyn."

"That you, Miss Evelyn?" came a cautious reply from somewhere above.

"It's me, Luke. Just showing our visitors around a bit."

"Well, all right," Luke drawled. "Thought the feller was by himself. Just about gave him a warning shot."

Miss Evelyn knew that by herself she would have been welcome at the cabin. But she understood how hard it was for the mountain people to trust outsiders. Miss Evelyn kept the group on the trail, away from Luke's cabin.

Miss Evelyn had not been born in these mountains. In fact, she had come from far-away California. When she graduated from college, she and her friend Elaine Polman had traveled through this area. They saw rough little shacks where entire families lived in one small room. They saw thin, hungry children in ragged clothes who didn't even own a pair of shoes. They saw people dying because they had no medicine to heal their sicknesses.

What broke their hearts the most, though, was meeting boys and girls who didn't know Jesus. "What hope do these people have," they asked themselves, "without Jesus?"

Evelyn and Elaine applied to the home missions board of the Brethren Church, and were sent to Clayhole, Kentucky. But they knew they would need a special kind of car that could handle the rough dirt roads full of potholes — and sometimes deep mud. The mission asked for help to buy a Jeep. All over the United States, girls in SMM clubs (see Mary Bauman pp. 19–23) heard about this need. They started putting their money together to send to the mission. Soon there was enough to buy the Jeep.

Evelyn and Elaine named their Jeep "JIM" to stand for Jesus Is Mine. Then they loaded it up and headed down to Clayhole.

The pastor of the church in Clayhole was glad to see them. Some men from a Brethren church had built a little apartment for them onto one side of Pastor Landrum's house. Evelyn and Elaine started teaching the Bible to the children in ten schools in the area. Soon they were teaching a thousand children each week! They would also plan special after-school activities for the children.

Evelyn and Elaine visited the children in their homes. They encouraged the families by helping them in whatever way they could.

One of the ways they helped was by working in the clothing room. That was where they stored the barrels and bundles of used clothing that people in different churches sent. The clothing was a wonderful help to the people of Clayhole who could not afford to buy new clothes when their old ones wore out.

Evelyn and Elaine would sort and organize the clothing to make it easier for people to find their size. While they worked, they kept their eyes open for something that would fit them, since they knew they wouldn't have money to buy new clothes when their own wore out. Evelyn seemed to find things she could use, but Elaine could never find anything that fit.

One day Elaine left the clothing room early—it was her turn to start supper. When Evelyn came home, she was hiding something behind her back. "I think you will like this," she told Elaine. Then she showed Elaine a sweater of her favorite colors. "Try it on," she said excitedly. Hardly daring to hope, Elaine pulled on the sweater. It fit perfectly!

Then she took a closer look. "I recognize this sweater!" she exclaimed. "Before I left home, I told my mother I didn't need or want it. She must have kept it, and now she has sent it to the mission!" They both laughed—Elaine finally had something that fit and looked good on her.

After three years in Clayhole, Elaine went home, and Miss Evelyn was asked to move to Dryhill. There she was the only missionary. She was responsible for all the church services, unless she could get a nearby pastor to come help. She visited people to find out what they needed and to tell them how to know Jesus. The little chapel at Dryhill was very special to Evelyn. Again, the SMM girls helped out by sending money for it. Evelyn made sure the chapel was painted white and green, SMM colors, in honor of the girls who had sacrificed their money to help provide a place for the people of Dryhill to worship.

Since most of the people in the area didn't use clocks, the chapel had a big silver bell that Evelyn rang when it was time for services. One time she wrote in a letter home, "We wish you could see the people as they come up and down the road as the big silver bell calls them to come and worship. Far up in some of the little 'hollers' folk have said they can hear the bell. Certainly they can never say, 'I never had a chance.'"

Miss Evelyn's home in Dryhill was along a creek called Hell-for-Certain. The creek lived up to its name—one day it flooded and her home was destroyed. She didn't let that stop her. Kind women in Brethren churches sent offerings to help build a new home for her near the chapel.

Sometimes the leaders of the mission board would say, "Miss Evelyn, maybe you shouldn't be here all alone. This isn't a safe place to be." She would always answer, "Jesus is mine. He will take care of me."

Miss Evelyn prayed for many years that a pastor would someday come to take care of the little mission church in Dryhill. Finally, in 1965, her prayers were answered. Leaving the people of Dryhill taken care of, she went to the island of St. Thomas in the Caribbean area, then to the island of Dominique. She threw her energy into teaching boys and girls in the Caribbean about Jesus.

Miss Evelyn suffered from diabetes. After 14 years in the Caribbean, she returned from her missionary service. Shortly after she came back home, she was eating with her relatives when she looked across the table and said, "Oh! I see two Uncle Luthers and two Aunt Nellies!" Her family took her to the hospital, where the doctors told them she'd had a stroke. She died May 17, 1979.

The Brethren Home Missions Council said in an article written after she died, "We are grateful for her life, dedicated talent, and faithful missionary service, a beautiful example for all of us to follow."

Questions for Discussion

1. In what ways did Miss Evelyn serve the people of Dryhill? Can you think of ways to serve others you know?

2. Who are some people in the Bible who showed compassion toward others? How did they do it?

3. Miss Evelyn helped people who were different from her. Do you know someone who is different from you? What can you do to show friendship to that person?

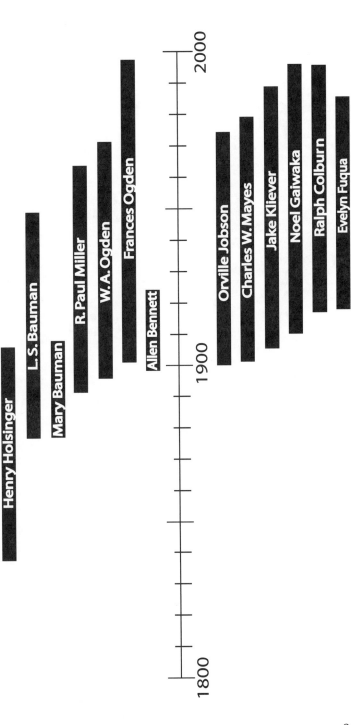

Heroes Timeline

Henry Holsinger
L. S. Bauman
Mary Bauman
R. Paul Miller
W. A. Ogden
Frances Ogden
Allen Bennett
Orville Jobson
Charles W. Mayes
Jake Kliever
Noel Gaiwaka
Ralph Colburn
Evelyn Fuqua

1800
1900
2000

Bibliography

Ankrum, Freeman. *A History of the Brethren Church,* Scottdale: The Herald Press

Beaver, Wayne. *God at Work in the Central African Republic*, n.d.

The Brethren Encyclopedia, Philadelphia: The Brethren Encyclopedia, 1983.

The Brethren Missionary, Ashland: Foreign Missionary Society of the Brethren Church

The Brethren Missionary Herald, Winona Lake: Brethren Missionary Herald Co.

Durnbaugh, Donald F. ed. *Meet the Brethren,* Philadelphia: Brethren Encyclopedia, Inc, 1995. 123 pages. (Brief history and present condition of the five largest Brethren groups)

Gribble, Florence Newberry. *Stranger Than Fiction.* Winona Lake: The Brethren Missionary Herald Co., 1949. 249 pages. (The life of Dr. Florence Gribble)

Gribble, Florence Newberry. *Undaunted Hope.* Winona Lake: BMH Books, 1984. 438 pages. (The life of James Gribble)

Hamilton, Benjamin A. *Gribble's Dream ... God's Design.* Winona Lake: BMH Books, 1987. 300 pages. (Historical presentation of the founding of the Brethren missionary work in Central African Republic)

Holsinger, Henry. *History of the Tunkers and The Brethren Church.* Oakland: Pacific Press, 1901.

Jobson, Orville D. *Conquering Oubangui-Chari For Christ.*
Winona Lake: Brethren Missionary Herald Co., 1957. 160
pages (History of the Early Years of the Brethren missionary
work in Central African Republic)

Julien, Tom. *Seize the Moment.* Winona Lake: Grace Brethren
International Missions, 2000. 132 pages.

Kent, Sr., Homer A. *Conquering Frontiers: A History of
the Brethren Church.* Revised ed. Winona Lake: Brethren
Missionary Herald, 1972. 245 pages.

Kinsley, Bob. *His Greatest Legacy.* Nappanee: Evangel Press,
1996. 95 pages. (The history of the Brethren Movement and
the "Dilemma of the 19th Century Brethren")

LIGHT, Long Beach: First Brethren Church of Long Beach,
May 21, 1965. (Church newsletter)

Plaster, David. *Finding Our Focus.* Winona Lake: BMH Books,
2003, 178 pages (A history of the Grace Brethren Church to 2003)

Ronk, Albert T. *History of the Brethren Church.* Ashland:
Brethren Publishing Co., 1968. 524 pages.

Significant Times, Winona Lake: Grace Brethren Foreign
Missions, Summer 1988. (Regular Newsletter)

Snyder, Ruth. *Estella Myers: Pioneer Missionary in Central
Africa.* Winona Lake: BMH Books, 1984. 167 pages. (The life
of Estella Myers)

Woman's Outlook, Ashland: The Brethren Church, 1933. p. 21
(Bi-monthly magazine)

The World Book Encyclopedia, Chicago: Field Enterprises
Educational Corp., 1961.

General References

Letters and pictures from private collections, phone calls, interviews with family members, associates, and friends, maps and atlases, RootsWeb.com - web page on Internet.

About the Contributors

Viki Rife directs communications for Women of Grace, the women's affiliate of the Fellowship of Grace Brethren Churches. She is also the National Director of SMM. Formerly head of publications for CE National, she was raised by missionary parents in Argentina. She has had a long-standing interest in journalism and served as editor of the Grace College student newspaper while studying journalism there. She and her husband John have three grown children and attend the Leesburg, Indiana, Grace Brethren Church, where she is active in youth and children's work, Hispanic ministries, and mentoring needy girls.

Bob Cover, Sr., is retired and lives in Warsaw, Indiana, with his wife Joene. They have been married for 50 years. Bob and his family served for ten years as missionaries in Argentina, where he pastored churches, managed a bookstore, and published the national church magazine, *El Heraldo.* After returning to the U.S., Cover became involved in Christian schools, serving as assistant director of the Midwest Association of Christian Schools International and as the principal and administrator of two Christian schools. He was also chaplain for a community hospital and a large nursing home.

Ashley Woodworth, who copy-edited the book and created most of the discussion questions, is a 2005 graduate of Grace College who was an editorial intern with Brethren Missionary Herald Co. and BMH Books during the spring semester, 2005. Originally from Waterloo, Indiana, she has written for the Grace College student newspaper, for several community newspapers, and for *FGBC World,* a publication for the Fellowship of Grace Brethren Churches. She is an honors diploma graduate of Lakewood Park Christian School.

Sarah Pratt, who created the sketches of the featured subjects and designed the cover, is a 2005 graduate of Grace

College, Winona Lake, IN, with an Illustration major. She lives in Crown Point, Indiana, and has a freelance illustration and graphic business.

Volume One

Volume One of *Heroes Who Live On*, published in 2002, is available from BMH Books and from CE National. It features the following Grace Brethren heroes: Alexander Mack, Florence Gribble, James Gribble, Estella Myers, Alva McClain, Russell Humberd, Homer Kent, Sr., Russell Barnard, Leo Polman, Harold and Ada Etling, Herman Hoyt, and Clyde Landrum.

Brethren Missionary Herald Company

The Brethren Missionary Herald Company (BMH) is the communication/publishing arm of the Fellowship of Grace Brethren Churches (FGBC), headquartered in Winona Lake, Indiana.

BMH's mission is "to nurture Great Commission teamwork among the people and churches of the FGBC by building bridges of communication."

BMH's bi-monthly periodical *FGBC World* is available online at www.fgbcworld.com and by mail free to anyone who requests it. Daily updates on the people and churches of the FGBC may be seen by clicking on "editor's blog."

A complete catalog of BMH books is available by mail, by calling 1-800-348-2756, or online at www.bmhbooks.com. In addition to literature with a specific interest in the FGBC, BMH is also the publisher of quality Christian materials for a general audience. Some of BMH's books for those with a specific interest in the Fellowship of Grace Brethren Churches include:

The Kent Collection. A series of 15 New Testament commentaries by Dr. Homer Kent, Jr., professor emeritus and former president of Grace College and Grace Theological Seminary.

The Greatness of the Kingdom, a significant treatment by Alva J. McClain, founding president of Grace College and Seminary.

Finding Our Focus by Dr. David Plaster. A history of the Grace Brethren Church which updates an earlier work by Dr. Homer A. Kent, Sr.

Additional works by Grace Brethren authors including John J. Davis, L. S. Bauman, Herman Hoyt, Tom Julien, and others.

BMH is also the publisher and distributor of the *Life's Most Important Question* tract with more than 4,000,000 now in print in several languages.

For a broader look at Brethren history, contact the Brethren Encyclopedia Project at The Brethren Encyclopedia, 313 Fairview Avenue, Ambler, PA 19002 or log onto www.brethrenencyclopedia.org.

CE National, which originated the Heroes Who Live On project, is directed by Ed Lewis. Its purpose is "to impact the church by serving as a catalyst for biblically accurate and culturally relevant ministries to children, youth and adults."

CE National may be contacted at P.O. Box 365, Winona Lake, Indiana, 46590, by calling (574) 267-6622, or by logging onto www. cenational.org.